It's Easy To Play 90s Film Songs.

Wise Publications
London / New York / Paris / Sydney / Copenhagen / Madrid

Exclusive Distributors:

Music Sales Limited
8/9 Frith Street, London W1V 5TZ, England.

Music Sales Pty Limited
120 Rothschild Avenue, Rosebery, NSW 2018, Australia.

Order No. AM956208
ISBN 0-7119-7833-6
This book © Copyright 1999 by Wise Publications.

Book design by Michael Bell Design.
Cover photograph courtesy of Rex Features.
Compiled by Nick Crispin.
Music arranged by Stephen Duro.
Music processed by Allegro Reproductions.

Music Sales' complete catalogue describes thousands of titles and
is available in full colour sections by subject, direct from Music Sales Limited.
Please state your areas of interest and send a cheque/postal order for £1.50 for postage to:
Music Sales Limited, Newmarket Road, Bury St. Edmunds, Suffolk IP33 3YB.

www.internetmusicshop.com

Your Guarantee of Quality:
As publishers, we strive to produce every book to the highest commercial standards.
The music has been freshly engraved and the book has been carefully designed to minimise awkward page turns and to make playing from it a real pleasure.
Particular care has been given to specifying acid-free, neutral-sized paper made from pulps which have not been elemental chlorine bleached.
This pulp is from farmed sustainable forests and was produced with special regard for the environment.
Throughout, the printing and binding have been planned to ensure a sturdy, attractive publication which should give years of enjoyment.
If your copy fails to meet our high standards, please inform us and we will gladly replace it.

Printed in the United Kingdom by
Caligraving Limited, Thetford, Norfolk.

All For Love
(The Three Musketeers)

Words & Music by Bryan Adams, Robert John 'Mutt' Lange & Michael Kamen

then there's a rea - son why___ I'll prove to you we be - long,___
then it's love you take___ I will de - fend, I will fight,___

___ I'll be the one that pro - tects___ you, from the wind and the
___ I'll be there when you need___ me, When hon - our's at

G

D/A   A   D   N.C.
rain,   from the hurt and the   pain.   Let's make it
stake,   this vow I will   make.   And it's

𝄋 G   Em⁷
all   for   one and all for   love   let the one you hold   be the one you

D/A   A   G   A   D
want,   the one you   need.   'Cause when it's   all for one it's one for

5

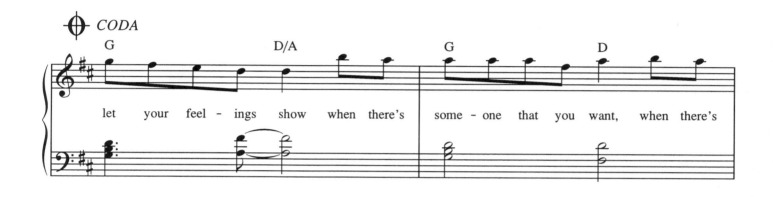

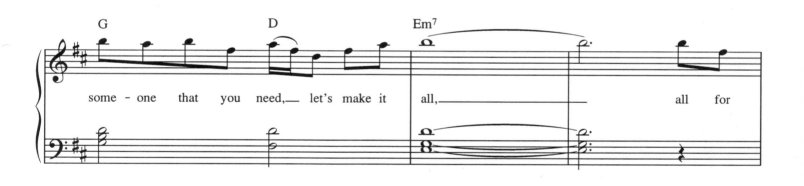

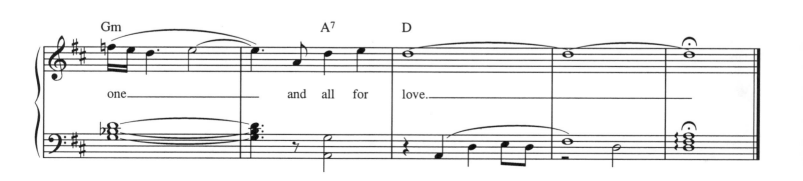

Change The World
(Phenomenon)

Words & Music by Tommy Sims, Gordon Kennedy & Wayne Kirkpatrick

Moderately

mf If I could reach the stars,
(Verse 2 see block lyric)
pull one down for you.

Shine it on my heart,

so you could see the truth.
Then this love I have in-side,

is ev-'ry-thing it seems,

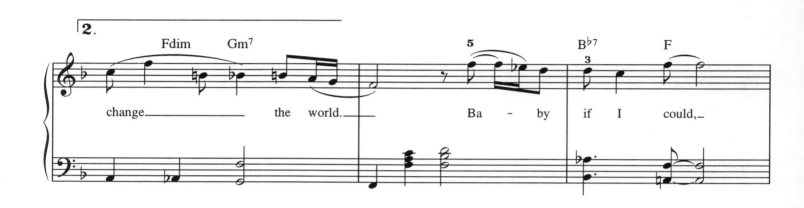

change_____ the world.____ Ba - by if I could,_

change_____ the world._____

D.S. al Coda

I can

CODA

change the world___ ba - by, if I could___ change the world___ ba - by,

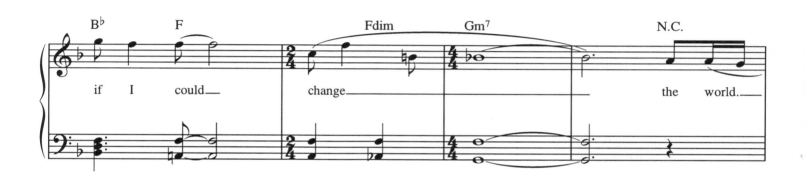

if I could___ change_____ the world.___

Verse 2:

If I could be king
Even for a day
I'd take you as my queen
I'd have it no other way.
And our love would rule
In this kingdom we have made.
Till then I'd be a fool,
Wishing for the day.

Have You Ever Really Loved A Woman?

(Don Juan de Marco)

Words & Music by Bryan Adams, Robert John "Mutt" Lange & Michael Kamen

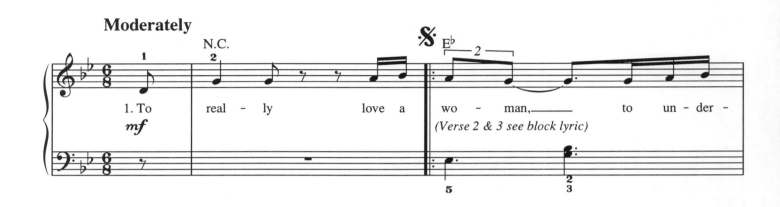

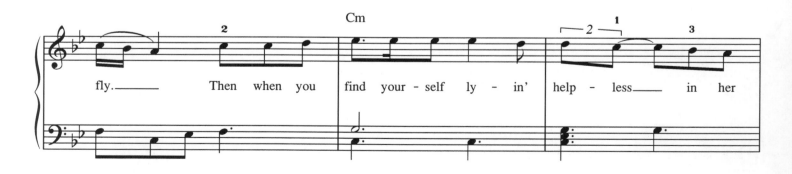

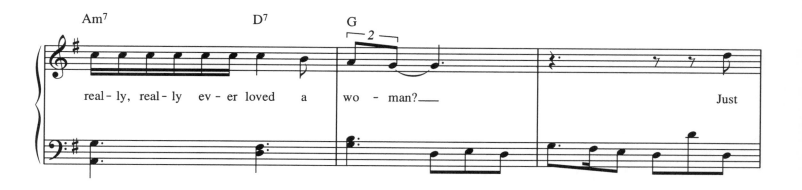

real-ly, real-ly ev-er loved a wo-man?____ Just

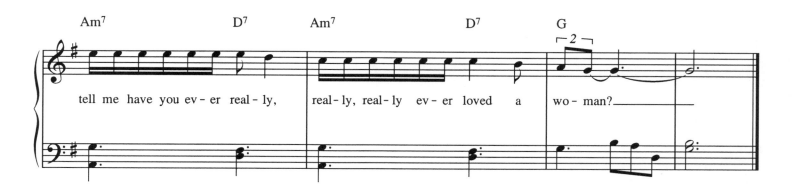

tell me have you ev-er real-ly, real-ly, real-ly ev-er loved a wo-man?____

Verse 2:

To really love a woman, let her hold you
Till you know how she needs to be touched.
You've gotta breathe her, really taste her,
Till you can feel her in your blood.
And when you can see your unborn children in her eyes,
You know you really love a woman.

When you love a woman
You tell her that she's really wanted.
When you love a woman
You tell her that she's the one.
She needs somebody to tell her
That you'll always be together
So tell me have you ever really,
Really, really loved a woman.

Verse 3:
Instrumental

Then when you find yourself
Lyin' helpless in her arms,
You know you really love a woman.

When you love a woman *etc.*

It Must Have Been Love
(Pretty Woman)

Words & Music by Per Gessle

Moderately

It must have been love_____ but it's ov - er now.__

1. Lay a whis - per__ on my pil - low,__ leave the win - ter__ on the
(Verse 2 see block lyric)

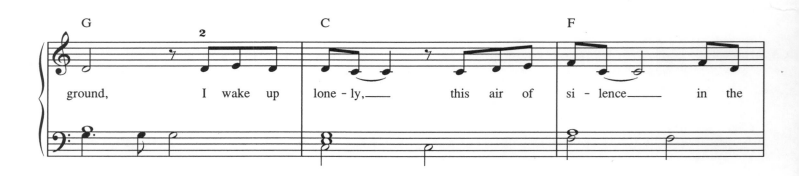

ground, I wake up lone - ly,__ this air of si - lence__ in the

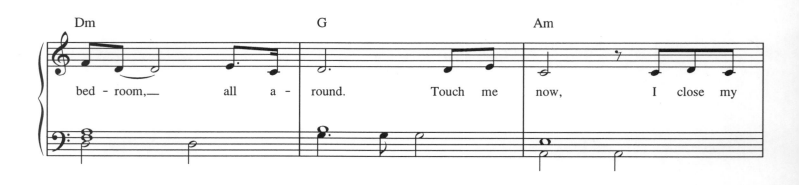

bed - room,__ all a - round. Touch me now, I close my

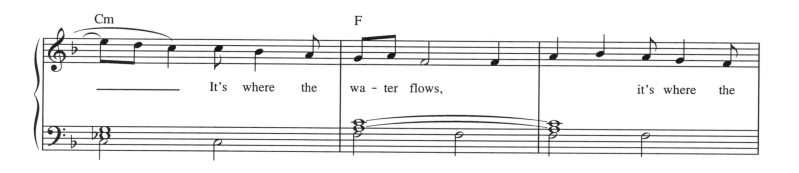

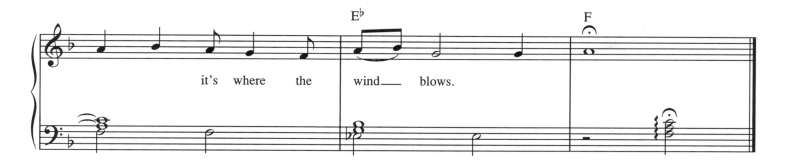

Verse 2:

Make believing we're together
That I'm sheltered by your heart.
But in and outside I turn to autumn
Like a teardrop in your palm.

And it's a hard winter's day
I dream away.

It must have been love but it's over now
It was all that I wanted, now I'm living without.
It must have been love but it's over now.
It's where the water flows,
It's where the wind blows.

Lovefool
(Romeo And Juliet)

Words & Music by Peter Svensson & Nina Persson

an – y – thing but   you._____

CODA

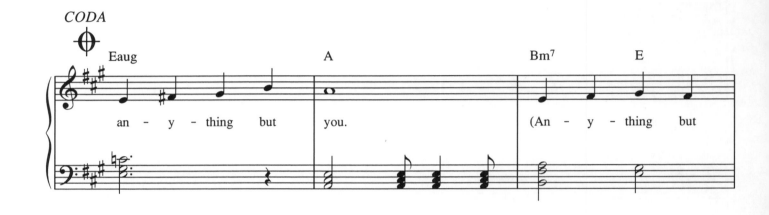

an – y – thing but   you.   (An – y – thing but

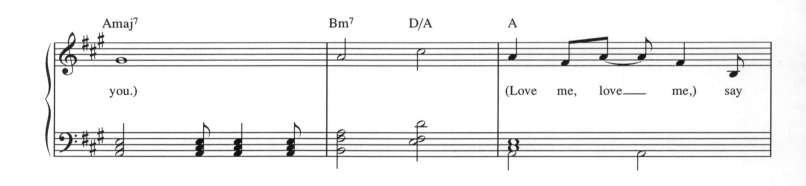

you.)   (Love   me,   love___ me,)   say

that   you   love   me.___   (Fool   me,   fool___ me,)   go   on   and   fool   me.

(Love me, love— me.) I know that you need me, I can't care a - bout

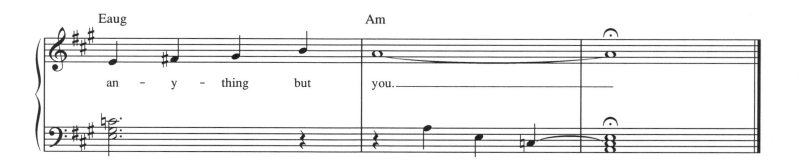

an – y – thing but you._____

Verse 2:

Mama tells me I shouldn't bother,
That I ought to stick to another man,
A man that surely deserves me.
But I think you do.

Verse 3:

Lately I have desp'rately pondered.
Spent my nights awake and I wonder
What I could have done in any other way
To make you stay.

Verse 4:

Reason will not lead to solution
I will end up lost in confusion.
I don't care if you really care
As long as you don't go.

Show Me Heaven
(Days Of Thunder)

Words & Music by Maria McKee, Jay Rifkin & Eric Rackin

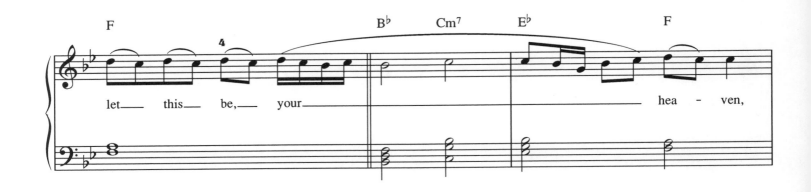

let___ this___ be,___ your___ hea - ven,

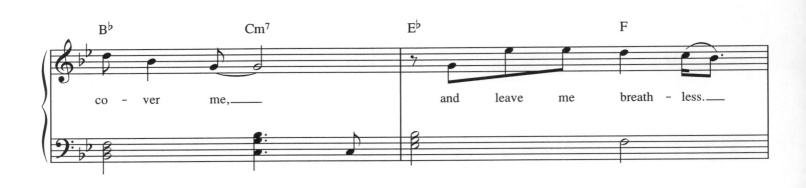

co - ver me,___ and leave me breath - less.___

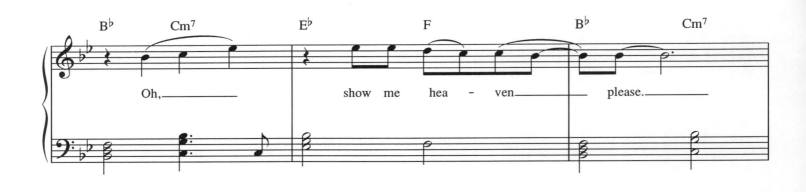

Oh,___ show me hea - ven___ please.___

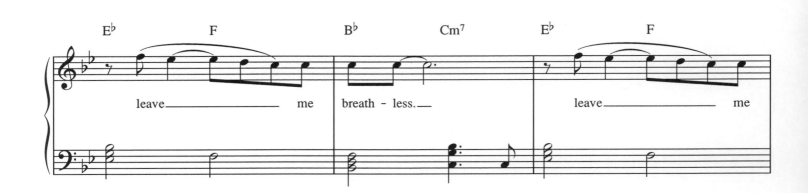

leave___ me breath - less.___ leave___ me

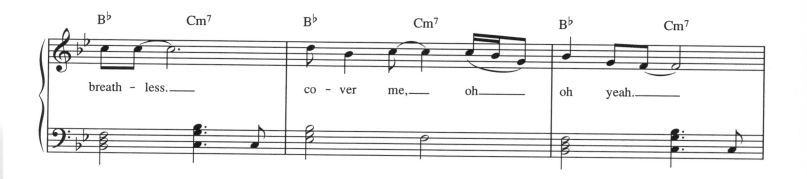

breath - less.___ co - ver me,___ oh_____ oh yeah.___

oh yeah.___

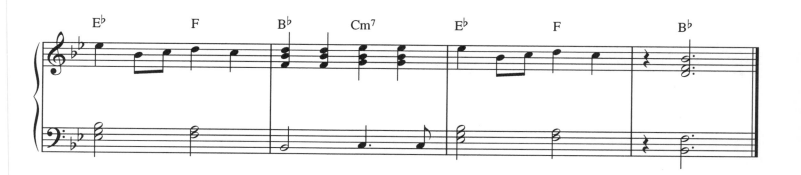

Verse 2:

Here I go, I'm shaking
Just like the breeze
Hey babe, I need your hand
To steady me
I'm not denying
I'm frightened as much as you
Though I'm barely touching you
I've shivers down my spine
And it feels divine.

Oh, show me heaven *etc.*

Son Of A Preacher Man
(Pulp Fiction)

Words & Music by John Hurley & Ronnie Wilkins

Moderately

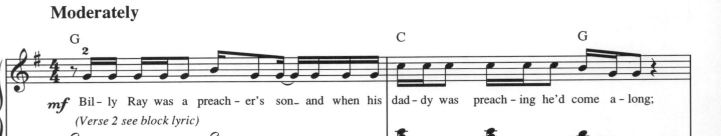

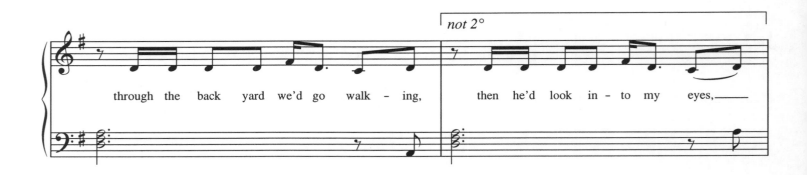

Verse 2:

Being good isn't always easy
No matter how hard I try.
When he started sweet talking to me,
He'd come and tell me everything is all right,
He'd kiss and tell me everything is all right,
Can't get away again tonight.

Female Of The Species
(Austin Powers: International Man Of Mystery)

Words & Music by Tommy Scott, James Edwards, Francis Griffiths & Andrew Parle

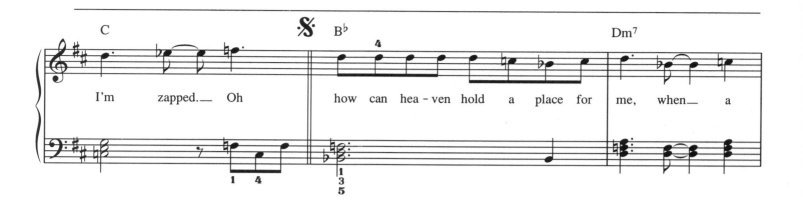

I'm zapped.___ Oh how can hea - ven hold a place for me, when___ a

girl like you has cast a spell on me? Oh___ how can hea - ven hold a place for

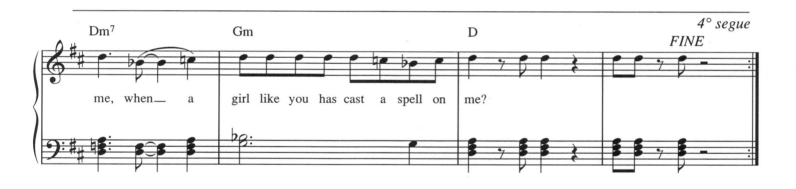

me, when___ a girl like you has cast a spell on me?

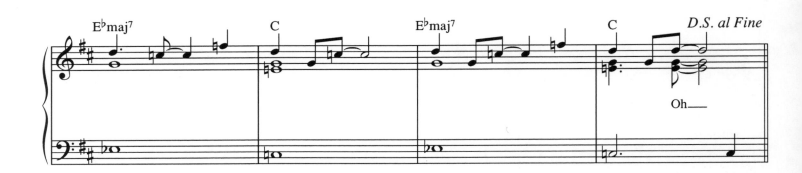

Verse 2:

Shock, shock, horror, horror, shock, shock, horror,
I'll shout myself hoarse for your supernatural force.
The female of the species
Is more deadly than the male.

Verse 3:

Frankenstein and Dracula have nothing on you,
Jekyll and Hyde join the back of the queue.
The female of the species
Is more deadly than the male.

Verse 4:

Oh she wants to conquer the world completely,
But first she'll conquer me discreetly.
The female of the species
Is more deadly than the male.

The Time Of Your Life
(A Bug's Life)

Words & Music by Randy Newman

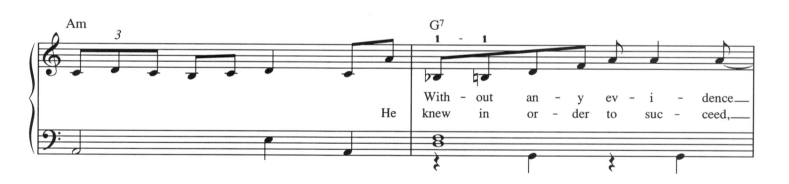

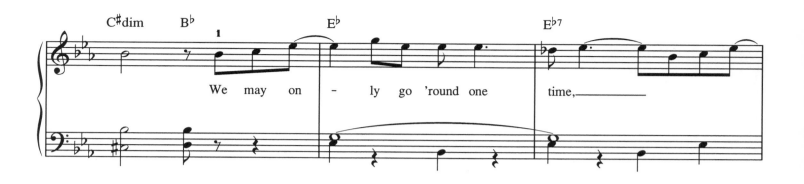

We may on - ly go 'round one time,

as far as I can tell. It's the time of your life,

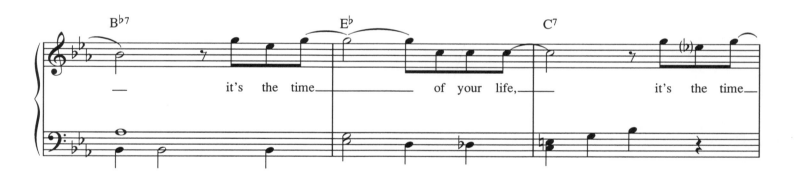

it's the time of your life, it's the time

of your life so live it well.

Turn Back Time
(Sliding Doors)

Words & Music by Soren Rasted, Claus Norreen, Johnny Pederson & Karsten Delgado

Moderately

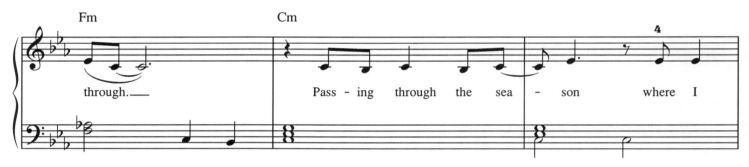

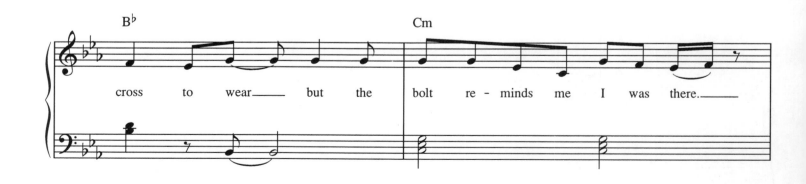

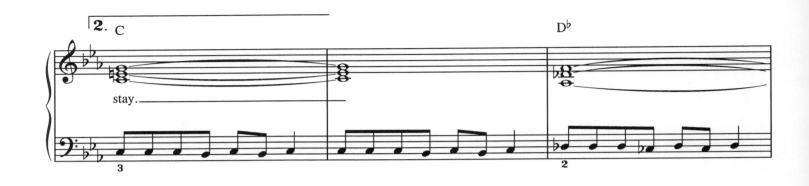

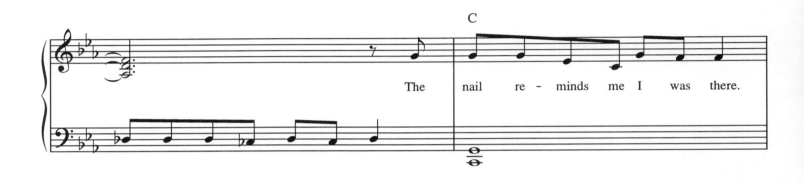

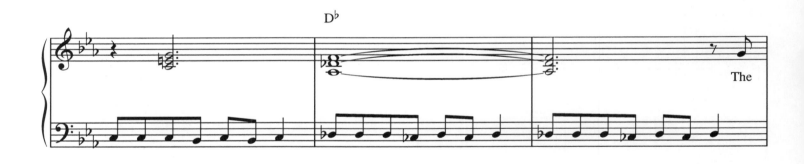

turn_____ back time._____ _____ If on-ly I had said what I_____ still__ hide__

_____ if on-ly I could turn_____ back time._____ _____ I would

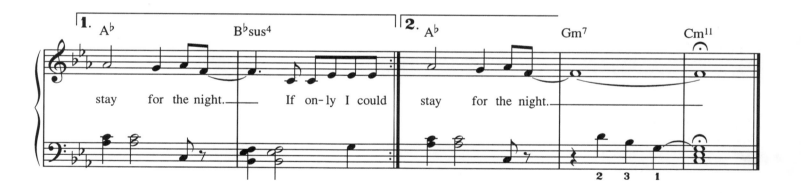

stay for the night.____ If on-ly I could stay for the night.____

Verse 2:

Claim your right to science
Claim your right to see the truth,
Though my pangs of conscience
Will drill a hole in you.

I've seen you coming like a thief in the night
I've seen it coming from the flash of your light
So give me strength to face this test of mine.

You Must Love Me
(Evita)

Music by Andrew Lloyd Webber
Lyrics by Tim Rice

Moderately

how do we keep____ all our pas - sions a - live as

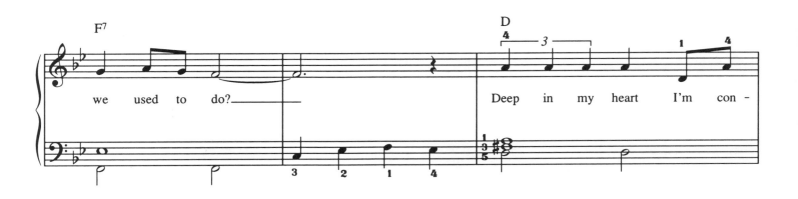

we used to do?____ Deep in my heart I'm con -

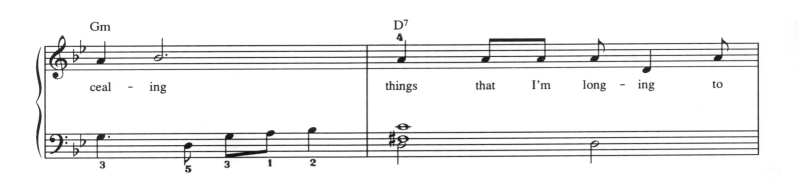

ceal - ing things that I'm long - ing to

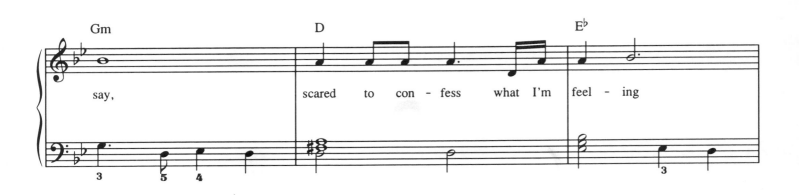

say, scared to con - fess what I'm feel - ing

fright - ened you'll slip a - way, you must love me,

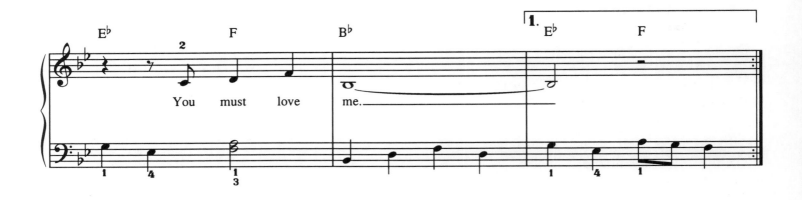

You must love me. ____

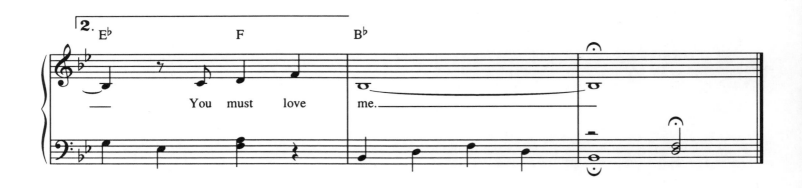

____ You must love me. ____

Verse 2: (Instrumental 8 bars)

Why are you at my side?
How can I be any use to you now?
Give me a chance and I'll let you see how
Nothing has changed.
Deep in my heart I'm concealing
Things that I'm longing to say,
Scared to confess what I'm feeling
Frightened you'll slip away,
You must love me.

More Great Music from the Silver Screen

Check out these other selected film titles for solo piano...

Aladdin: Piano Solos

Seven great Disney songs including 'Arabian Nights',
'One Jump Ahead' and 'A Whole New World'.
*Order No. HLD00292018 (Easy piano edition with full-colour
illustrations from the film also available: Order No. HLD00222555)*

Jane Austen: The Music

Solo piano arrangements of music from
Sense And Sensibility and Pride And Prejudice.
Order No. AM944592

Beauty And The Beast: Easy Piano

Easy piano arrangements of songs from the popular Disney film,
complete with lyrics and chord symbols.
Order No. HLD00110003

Fantasia: Piano Solos

An outstanding matching folio to the Disney landmark movie. Includes
arrangements of 15 famous classical pieces as well as full-colour
illustrations and six pages of background text about the movie.
Order No. HLD00292006
(Easy piano edition also available: Order No. HLD00490553)

Film Themes Of The Nineties

Music from seven top movie scores of the Nineties specially
arranged for solo piano by Jack Long. Includes 'The English Patient',
'Mission: Impossible', 'The Nightmare Before Christmas', 'Schindler's List',
'Sense And Sensibility', 'The Silence Of The Lambs' and 'Toy Story'.
Order No. AM952897

Film Themes Piano Solos

Full piano solo arrangements by Cyril Ornadel of 20 classic film themes.
Includes 'Chariots Of Fire', 'Lawrence Of Arabia' and 'Star Wars'.
Order No. AM90204

Selections From Forrest Gump

Twenty-two songs from the movie, arranged for easy piano
with lyrics and chord symbols.
Order No. AM938091

I Can Play That! Film Themes

The easiest ever piano arrangements of 13 screen hits,
including 'How Deep Is Your Love', 'GoldenEye',
'Circle Of Life' and 'Kiss From A Rose'.
Order No. AM936947

It's Easy To Play Movie Music

Simplified piano arrangements of 19 popular film and TV themes.
Screen hits include 'Big Spender', 'Eternally' and 'Over The Rainbow'.
Order No. AM953865

Jurassic Park: Piano Solos

Themes from the blockbuster movie
by John Williams, arranged for solo piano.
Includes colour photographs from the film.
Order No. AM91557

The Lion King: Piano Solos

Seven songs from the movie including 'Circle Of Life',
'This Land', 'Can You Feel The Love Tonight' and
'Be Prepared'.
Order No. HLD00292060

Michael Nyman: The Piano

Original compositions for solo piano from the
award-winning film. Play along with the music using the
Midi Disk or just listen to the performance by Jane Jackson.
*Order Nos. CH60871 (Book only), OM23495 (Disk only),
CH61065 (Book and Disk).*

The Music Of Michel Legrand

Sixteen outstanding melodies by France's leading
film composer arranged as piano solos. Includes
'The Windmills Of Your Mind', and 'The Summer Knows'.
Order No. AM25727

Oliver! Easy Piano

Twelve songs arranged for easy piano with lyrics.
Includes 'Oom-Pah-Pah', 'Where Is Love?'
and 'Pick A Pocket Or Two'.
Order No. LK56187

Pocahontas: Easy Piano

Beautiful full-colour illustrations and easy piano
arrangements from the popular Disney film.
Order No. HLD00316002

Rodgers And Hammerstein Anthology

Thirty-nine of their greatest songs arranged for easy piano,
including 'Climb Ev'ry Mountain', 'Getting To Know You',
'Some Enchanted Evening' 'Edelweiss', and
'You'll Never Walk Alone'.
Order No. HLW00366008

Schindler's List: Piano Solos

Thought provoking music by John Williams from the film.
Order No. AM92669

The Sound Of Music: Piano Selection

A medley of songs from one of the most popular of films ever!
Order No. HLW00312713